FROGS

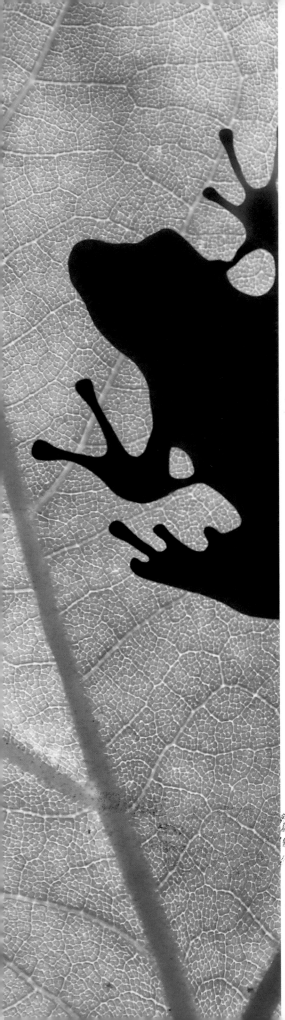

LIVING WILD

Published by Creative Education
P.O. Box 227, Mankato, Minnesota 56002
Creative Education is an imprint of The Creative Company
www.thecreativecompany.us

Design and production by Mary Herrmann
Art direction by Rita Marshall
Printed in the United States of America

Photographs by Alamy (Accent Alaska.com, John Cancalosi, F1online digitale Bildagentur GmbH, Buddy Mays), Conservation International (S. D. Biju/Lost Frogs), Dreamstime (Grecu Mihail Alin, Guido Amrein, Rob Corbett, Alexandre Fagundes De Fagundes, Janpietruszka, Bill O\'neill, Timurk), Guy Stuff, nefertari-egyptian.blogspot.com (SSK), Shutterstock (Brandon Alms, Anneka, Ryan M. Bolton, Gerald A. DeBoer, Gilles Decruyenaere, EcoPrint, Dirk Ercken, formiktopus, Elliotte Rusty Harold, Andy Heyward, Patryk Kosmider, Eduard Kyslynskyy, David W. Leindecker, Luis Louro, LuckyKeeper, Number One, Rat007, Dr. Morley Read, Jason Patrick Ross, Uryadnikov Sergey, Steffen Foerster Photography, Ilias Strachinis, Albie Venter), SuperStock (imagebroker.net, Minden Pictures), Veer (kikkerdirk), Wikipedia (C.C. Austin/E.N. Rittmeyer, John Gerrard Keulemans/Alfred Russel Wallace, LiquidGhoul, Arthur Rackham, Kikuchi Yosai)

Library of Congress Cataloging-in-Publication Data
Gish, Melissa.
Frogs / by Melissa Gish.
p. cm. — (Living wild)
Includes index.
Summary: A look at frogs, including their habitats, physical characteristics such as their webbed feet, behaviors, relationships with humans, and protected status in the world today.
ISBN 978-1-60818-287-9
1. Frogs—Juvenile literature. I. Title.

QL668.E2G47 2013
597.8'9—dc23   2012023243

First Edition
9 8 7 6 5 4 3 2 1

C CREATIVE EDUCATION

FROGS

Melissa Gish

An afternoon shower has drenched the
rainforest surrounding Costa Rica's

Toro River. A barely visible strawberry poison dart tadpole flops in a bead of water on a leaf.

An afternoon shower has drenched the rainforest surrounding Costa Rica's Toro River. A barely visible strawberry poison dart tadpole flops in a bead of water on a leaf. Its father has been standing guard as the tadpole hatched from its egg. No bigger than a paper clip, with black legs and a brilliant red body, the adult frog shimmers like a tiny ruby. The frog squats down so that the tadpole can wriggle atop its back. With its offspring firmly stuck to its back, the male frog climbs a tree, followed by the tadpole's mother. The male drops the tadpole into a bromeliad, a plant that holds enough standing water in its center vessel for the tadpole to survive. The female frog then deposits an infertile egg into the plant—food for the tadpole. Their job done, the frogs disappear into the foliage, leaving their young to develop on its own in the forest.

■ **American Bullfrog** North America

■ **Red-eyed Treefrog** Central America

■ **Blue Poison Dart Frog** Suriname and Brazil

■ **Common Reed Frog** eastern and central Africa

■ **Australian Green Tree Frog** Australia and New Guinea

■ **Common Frog** Europe

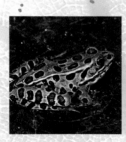

■ **Leopard Frog** western United States, Mexico

■ **Wood Frog** Alaska, Canada, northeastern United States

More than 5,000 frog species are found throughout the world on all continents except Antarctica. Creatures that need moisture, many frogs inhabit tropical rainforests, marshes, wooded areas, grasslands near water sources, and other such environments. Some can even survive in the desert. The colored squares represent common locations of eight species.

GOING GREEN

Frogs are members of the Amphibia class of animals, which means they live part of their lives in water and part on land. Like other amphibians, such as toads, newts, and salamanders, frogs have been **adapting** to constantly changing conditions on Earth for about 250 million years—long before many commonly known dinosaurs appeared. Frogs can be found on every continent on Earth except Antarctica, and they vary greatly in size. The smallest frogs in the world, two species in the genus *Paedophryne*, were discovered as recently as 2011 in Papua New Guinea. At about 0.35 inches (9 mm) in length, it would take four of them to cover a penny, making them the smallest four-legged **vertebrates** on the planet. Growing to 12 inches (30 cm) in length, the American bullfrog is the largest frog in North America, but west-central Africa's goliath frog is the world's largest. It grows up to 35 inches (89 cm) long and weighs up to 8 pounds (3.6 kg).

Adult frogs have bulging eyes situated on top of a wide, flat head that is attached directly to the body with no neck. Their bodies are soft, having no ribs and no

Paedophryne amauensis young hatch as "hoppers," or miniature versions of adult frogs, instead of tadpoles.

Like other tree frogs, the glass frog of South America may lose its suctioning grip if its climbing surface is too wet.

The male Darwin's frog of Chile and Argentina carries its tadpoles in its mouth and remains close to froglets until they are full-grown.

more than eight bones in the back. With the exception of the marsupial frog of South America, frogs have no teeth in their lower jaw, but most species have tiny teeth that line the upper jaw. A sticky tongue—up to two inches (5 cm) long in some species—is attached to the front part of the mouth in a way that allows the tongue to shoot out of the mouth rapidly, capture prey with a gluey hold, and pull the prey back into the mouth in one quick movement. Frogs' back legs are longer and more muscular than their front legs, and frogs have no tail.

Frogs move mostly by hopping rather than walking, and specialized hip and shoulder joints act as shock absorbers to prevent injury when frogs land. Frogs can hop great distances. The Australian rocket frog can leap 50 times its own body length—a distance of more than 6 feet (1.8 m). All frogs have four toes on their front limbs and five toes on their back limbs. With the exception of some species of tree frog, most frogs have **webbed** feet. Frogs that spend more time on land than in the water typically have less webbing between their toes than frogs that are primarily **aquatic**. Instead of webbing, most species of tree frog have sticky disks, called toepads, on

There is a crease down the middle of a frog's tongue, which classifies it as being cleft—just like a human's tongue.

It takes only a few minutes for a frog to shed and devour its skin during the nearly weekly ritual of exuviation.

the bottom tips of their toes to aid in climbing plants and trees.

All frogs have loose skin that must remain moist. The skin is permeable, meaning that water and gases can pass through it. The skin on a frog's underside is particularly thin, which allows the frog to soak up moisture from the surface on which it sits. Frogs can also take in oxygen and expel waste material through their skin. Frogs shed and re-grow their skin regularly in a process called exuviation. Using their feet to rub off dead skin and push it forward over their heads, frogs then eat their discarded skin. The top layer of frog skin, called the epidermis, is generally clear. Layers of skin underneath may be colored gray or brown, and some frog species have yellow and black layers that blend together to give the frogs' skin a green or blue appearance. Many frog species can change color. Beneath the epidermis of color-changing frogs is a layer of skin covered with chromatophores, which are tiny sacs containing black **pigment**. Each chromatophore is attached to a nerve and muscle. When the frog feels cold, its brain sends a signal along the nerve to tell the muscle to contract, and then the chromatophores turn dark.

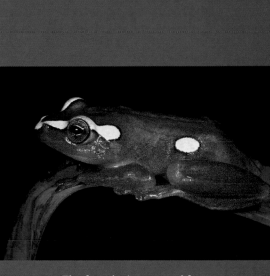

The female Argus reed frog is usually reddish with bright spots, while the male is often greenish in color.

Argus reed frogs are among only a handful of frog species whose males and females sport different colorations.

The most abundant frog species in Alaska, the wood frog is also the state amphibian of New York.

The blue poison dart frog is solitary except for about two weeks a year, when mating pairs guard their eggs until the tadpoles hatch.

When the frog feels warm, the chromatophores stretch and thin out, making the frog appear lighter-colored.

As amphibians, frogs are ectothermic animals, meaning that their bodies depend on external factors for warmth or cooling off and that their body temperatures change with the environment. In the morning and late afternoon, frogs warm their bodies in the sun. At midday, when the sun's heat becomes stronger, they retreat to shady areas or sink underwater to prevent overheating. Depending on the season and climate, many frogs are highly active at night. In northern climates, many frogs **hibernate** through cold winters. The wood frog, which is the only frog that lives north of the Arctic Circle, does more than hibernate—it freezes solid. At the first sign of freezing weather, the wood frog, buried under leaf litter, undergoes a transformation. The frog's body produces a special sugar that is circulated to all the cells. This fluid works like antifreeze, protecting the frog's eyes, skin, and internal organs from damaging ice crystals. Once the process is complete, the frog's heart stops beating—its blood is frozen solid. The frog can remain in this state for weeks or months—until spring arrives and warmer temperatures trigger the frog's heart to begin

The blue poison dart frog, popular as a pet, is one of Earth's most vulnerable species in the wild today.

The Wallace's flying frog was named after the biologist, Alfred Russel Wallace, who identified it.

Reinwardt's tree frogs and Wallace's flying frogs use their parachute-like webbed feet to glide through the air from branch to branch.

pumping warm blood again, thawing out the frog's body. It takes about 10 hours, but the frog recovers with no harm done. Scientists remain baffled by the wood frog's ability to survive this process.

Frogs and toads are often confused with each other. Many animals that are called toads, such as the Asian spadefoot toad and the Majorcan midwife toad, are actually frogs. In the order Anura, which contains both frogs and toads, only members of the family Bufonidae— about 500 species—are true toads. All the other animals in the order Anura—more than 5,400 known species— are frogs, and they account for nearly 90 percent of all amphibians. Frogs and toads are different physically. Toads have fatter bodies and drier skin than frogs, and as walking, land-dwelling animals, toads have clawed toes rather than webbed feet. Toads' eyes are more forward-facing than frogs', and, unlike most frogs, toads do not have teeth. Also, with the exception of 13 species of toad found only in Tanzania that give birth to live offspring, both frogs and toads lay eggs in water; however, while frogs lay their eggs in sticky clusters, toads lay their eggs in long strands on the leaves of water plants.

Fowler's toad, a frog relative, is found in most parts of the eastern U.S. except southern Florida.

OLD POND

Old Pond
frogs jumped in
sound of water

by Matsuo Basho (1644–94)

CALLING ALL FROGS

Frogs eat nearly anything, but feeding habits vary by species. The Orinoco lime tree frog feeds exclusively on insects, while the Forasini's spiny reed frog seeks out the eggs of other frogs. The edible frog of central Europe eats **larvae** underwater, and the barking tree frog, common in the southeastern United States, hunts crickets. The Indian green frog is the only known leaf-eating frog, with vegetation making up nearly 80 percent of its diet. And the giant bullfrog of southern Africa eats lizards, snakes, mice, and even other frogs. Most frogs snatch prey with their tongue and then use their front feet to stuff the prey into their mouths—usually while it is still alive. Frogs do not chew their meals. Teeth or toothlike bony projections in the upper jaw work food into the back of the mouth and help frogs swallow their meals whole. The African clawed frog has neither tongue nor teeth. This frog uses its hind claws to tear apart its prey and its front feet to shove food down its throat.

Most frogs are territorial, meaning they guard a selected area of land or water where they regularly hunt

Male African bullfrogs weigh up to four pounds (1.8 kg), but females of the species are only about half that size.

American bullfrogs recognize each other's calls, ignoring familiar neighbors but becoming aggressive upon hearing newcomers.

Australian green tree frogs are also called White's tree frogs for John White, a British surgeon who described them in 1790.

for food. Some frogs share territories, while others defend their private spaces fiercely, driving intruders away. With the exception of various tailed frog species in North America and New Zealand, all male frogs communicate vocally with each other to announce their location relative to other frogs' territories, warn off intruders, and attract mates. In some species, such as the nearly 30 species of whipping frog from China and Southeast Asia, females also vocalize. Commonly classified as croaking, frog vocalizations include a wide range of sounds, from chirps and trills to whistles, buzzes, and hums as well as grunts, groans, and clicks. The bullfrog honks like a goose, the common coquí sings like a songbird, and the Australian green tree frog squeaks when touched. Each frog species emits a sound unique to that species, and research has determined that sounds made by frogs of the same species may vary slightly, depending on the geographical location of the frog—much like people who live in the same country may have different ways of speaking the same language in different regions.

Frogs produce their croaks by forcing air through the **larynx**. With the exception of alarm calls that are emitted

while jumping away from a predator or human, all frog sounds are made while the frogs' mouths are closed. Most frogs have one or two elastic **membranes**, called vocal sacs, which stretch like a balloon under the lower jaw or a pair of balloons on each corner of the mouth or side of the body. These sacs amplify the frog's croaking sound, making its calls audible from more than a mile (1.6 km) away. The moaning frog and several of its close relatives in Australia have no vocal sacs. These frogs have huge mouth cavities that increase the intensity of the frog's sound, like the

Both male and female frogs possess vocal sacs, but these organs are usually more developed in the males.

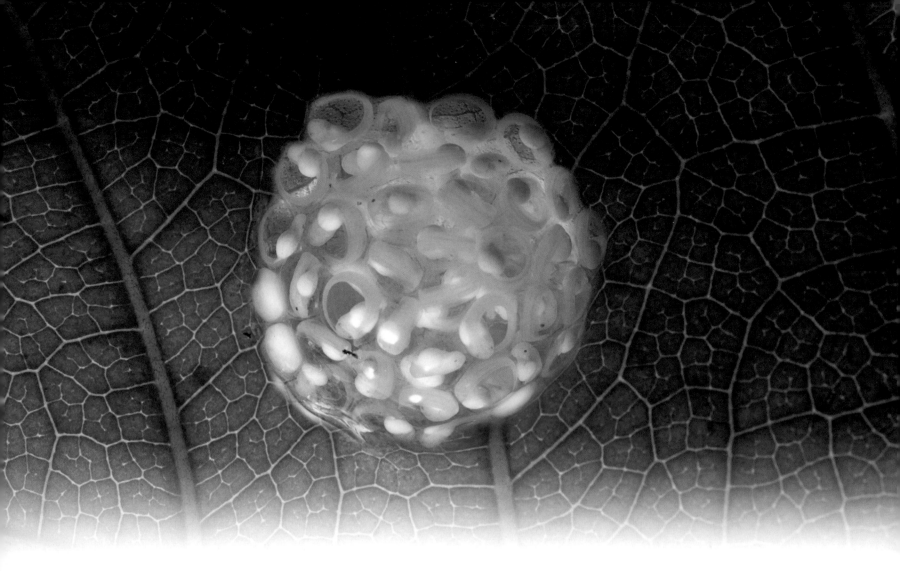

Frog eggs are covered with three layers of jelly coating over the course of the egg-laying process.

beating of a large drum. The Surinam toad (actually a frog) of South America and the African clawed frog can hear and vocalize underwater, and the concave-eared torrent frog of China communicates ultrasonically, making high-pitched noises that humans are incapable of hearing.

Like most of their amphibian relatives—toads, salamanders, newts, and caecilians (limbless, tropical creatures)—frogs reproduce by laying eggs in a watery environment. The mating behavior of frogs is as varied as the thousands of frog species themselves, but some aspects are fairly universal. First, a male vocalizes to attract females. When he selects a mate, the male jumps onto the female's back and clings to her in a posture called amplexus as he fertilizes her eggs. Frog eggs are protected by a clear, sticky substance called a jelly coat. Some species, such as wood frogs, lay one egg at a time, while others, such as bullfrogs, lay up to 20,000 eggs in a mass. Among foam nest frogs, up to 20 males work together to kick up gobs of sticky foam on tree branches for the female to lay her eggs. The nest then hardens to protect the developing offspring. Depending on the species, frogs may lay eggs in vegetation on the water's edge, on submerged pond grass, in floating nets, or on the underside of leaves. Giant monkey frogs of the Amazon lay eggs on leaves that hang six feet (1.8 m) above water. When the young hatch, they fall into the water.

Amphibians are the only vertebrates that begin life in a larval stage. Once frog eggs hatch—which can take a week to several months, depending on the species— tadpoles emerge. Tadpoles are fully aquatic, breathing through gills as fish do and equipped with a tail for propulsion. Clinging to vegetation with their sticky

Surinam toads drift like leaves in the water as a form of camouflage to hide from predators.

Surinam toad females' eggs are embedded on their backs for 77 to 136 days, when young emerge as fully developed toads.

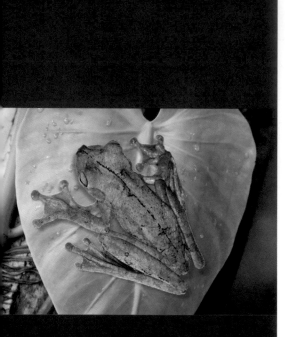

Male gladiator frogs of Ecuador use the sharp spurs on each front foot when fighting over territory and mating rights.

mouthparts, newly hatched tadpoles continue to absorb **nutrients** leftover from their eggs for the first week to 10 days of life. Then they begin to swim around and feed on algae. All tadpoles are herbivorous in the early stages of development, but some, such as the seven species of spadefoot toad, later become carnivorous, feeding on tiny organisms and even each other. In most frog species, skin begins to grow over the gills within a few weeks, and the tadpoles' teeth erupt. Several weeks later, legs emerge. Some frog species may retain their gills and tails and continue to be mostly aquatic for several months, fully maturing after 12 to 16 months. Other species may become froglets between the tadpole and adult stages, retaining a portion of their tail for several weeks. Because their lives are perilous, frogs in the wild rarely survive more than 2 or 3 years, but captive frogs often live more than 10 years—some captive tree frogs have lived as long as 18 years.

Frogs feed on insects and small vertebrates, and they themselves provide food for larger animals such as snakes, birds, and small mammals. In addition, tadpoles and froglets are preyed upon by fish, crustaceans,

and adult frogs. **Camouflage** is generally a frog's best defense. Wood frogs blend in with leaf litter, and canyon tree frogs match the black-and-white granite rock in their environment. Some frogs, such as poison dart frogs, protect themselves by advertising their toxicity with bright colors and bold patterns, called aposematic (*a-poh-sih-MA-tik*) coloring. Poisonous secretions on most poison dart frogs' bodies can kill anything—including a human—that touches or tastes the frog.

The mint poison dart frog generates the toxic substance it secretes through its skin from the ants that it consumes.

Frogs appear on wooden totem poles created by many Indian tribes of the American Pacific Northwest.

IT'S EASY BEING GREEN

Japanese artist Kikuchi Yosai depicted Ono no Michikaze in this early 19th-century drawing.

In **cultures** the world over, frogs are symbols of birth and rejuvenation, so they are also associated with many creation stories. The Tlingit, the native people of Canada's Pacific coast, tell how Raven asked Frog to get some sand from the bottom of the ocean, which he used to create the dry land. And in Australia, New Zealand, and surrounding islands, people play music to encourage frogs to croak, which they believe will bring rain. The sound of the didgeridoo, a wooden musical instrument played by blowing air through it, is modeled after the groaning of frogs that signals the coming rain.

A famous Japanese story tells of Ono no Tofu, an artist who failed to succeed in his work seven times and was about to give up. One day he saw a frog trying to leap up to grab a tree branch. Seven times the frog leaped and failed. But on the eighth attempt, the frog made it. This inspired Ono no Tofu to try again. This time he succeeded and became a famous artist. The tale is based on the experiences of Ono no Michikaze, who lived in the 10th century A.D. and is considered the father of Japanese calligraphy art. In

Madagascar's tomato frog secretes a milky substance that can cause allergic reactions in humans who touch it.

2000, a Japanese province issued a postage stamp depicting Michikaze watching the leaping frog.

The ancient Egyptians believed all life emerged from a prehistoric swamp, so frogs were associated with the cycle of creation and death. Followers of the Ogdoad, who were four male-female pairs of gods and goddesses first worshiped about 4,100 years ago, depicted the males as having frogs' heads and the females as having snakes' heads. It was believed they made the Nile River flow and the sun rise each day.

About 1,500 years later, a female Ogdoad named Heqet, the water goddess, emerged. Pictured with a frog head, she was associated with frogs, and followers believed that Heqet and her frogs presided over fertility and birth. Frog charms were worn on necklaces to promote fertility, and the dead were buried with the charms to aid their transformation in the afterlife. Frogs and tadpoles were also used to symbolize certain words and sounds in the Egyptian writing system.

In ancient Greece, the frog was believed to have once been a joyous and carefree creature. A fable by Aesop, the legendary Greek storyteller, recounts how the frogs asked the god Zeus to send them a frog king to rule over them.

Ancient Egyptian relief sculptures depict the frog-headed Heqet holding an ankh, a symbol for the "key of life."

Zeus dropped a log into the frogs' pond, but the frogs were not satisfied with this thing that simply sat in the middle of their pond and did not move. They begged Zeus for a living ruler. Zeus then sent a stork to the pond. The stork began gobbling up the frogs. The remaining frogs hid from the stork, grumbling in regret for not having appreciated the freedom they once enjoyed in the pond.

In Mesoamerica, the Maya considered frogs to be the musicians of the rain god, Chaac, and the creatures were thus associated with the emergence of plants and the birth of animals in springtime. The life cycle of the frog was taken to be symbolic of the cycle of life and death experienced by all living things. In the ancient Mesoamerican ruins of Cholula, in southern Mexico, archaeologists discovered a

Arthur Rackham's 19th-century illustration for "The Frog Prince" emphasizes the princess's distaste for the frog.

variety of artifacts depicting frogs, including carved clubs, bowls, and **fetishes** nearly 3,000 years old.

In medieval Europe, frogs were traditionally viewed much differently than in other parts of the world. Believed to be in league with the devil and the companions of witches, frogs were considered unclean, unlucky, and even deadly. Artwork and stories linking frogs and witchcraft include the famous conjuring scene in William Shakespeare's play *Macbeth*, which contains the lines "For a charm of powerful trouble, / Like a hell-broth boil and bubble... / Eye of newt and toe of frog, / Wool of bat and tongue of dog." Much of Europe's prejudices against frogs can be traced to the biblical story of the Plagues of Egypt from the book of Exodus, in which God sent swarms of frogs to overrun Egypt as a means of convincing the pharaoh to free the Hebrew slaves.

A frog is the central character in the famous Brothers Grimm fairy tale "The Frog Prince." In the original story, published in the 1812 book *Children's and Household Tales*, a princess encounters a frog who tries to convince her that he is a prince transformed by an evil spell. The princess, harboring a traditional European prejudice against frogs, is horrified and throws the frog against the wall. This violent act breaks the spell, and the frog turns back into a prince. Later writers, more sympathetic toward frogs, changed the tale's ending—at first the princess had to let the frog sleep on her pillow, but later, a kiss was needed to transform the frog into a prince.

The famous American writer Mark Twain got his start with a story about a frog that was trained to jump higher than any other. "The Celebrated Jumping Frog of Calaveras County" charmed readers in 1865 and continues

A small amount of water is often enough for many species of tree frog tadpoles to develop in the rainforest.

Majorcan midwife toad tadpoles, named for their Mediterranean island habitat, stop swimming when viperine snakes are nearby.

Kermit the Frog made his first appearance as a balloon in the Macy's Thanksgiving Day Parade in 1977.

to be included in short story collections around the world today. Capturing an image of peaceful country life, Beatrix Potter's book *The Tale of Mr. Jeremy Fisher* tells the story of a frog who sets out for a day of fishing and, upon encountering a number of unexpected obstacles, comes to appreciate his quiet existence. Modern stories about frogs include a series of books about two best friends, Frog and Toad, written and illustrated by Arnold Lobel. The award-winning collection has remained in print since the first book, *Frog and Toad Are Friends*, came out in 1970.

In 1955, cartoonist Chuck Jones created Michigan J. Frog, a singing, dancing frog who first appeared in the cartoon *One Froggy Evening* and has since become the logo for Warner Bros. Television. Also in 1955, puppeteer Jim Henson created perhaps the world's most famous amphibian, Kermit the Frog. Kermit first appeared on a local Washington, D.C., television show called *Sam and Friends*. From there, he joined *Sesame Street* and went on to star in *The Muppet Show* as well as dozens of television specials and feature films. Kermit later earned a star on the Hollywood Walk of Fame, and the U.S. Postal Service even issued a stamp commemorating his 50th birthday in 2005.

Many architectural remnants depicting the rain god Chaac appear in the ancient Mayan city of Uxmal near Mérida, Mexico.

Crab-eating frogs can tolerate salty mangrove swamps because of an ability to flush excess salt from their bodies.

CLINGING TO THE EDGE

F rogs have survived countless earthquakes, volcanoes, floods, and other massive geological and climatic changes that have reshaped life on our planet for 250 million years. But in recent decades, frogs have fallen victim to a number of environmental pressures that, intensified by human activity, threaten to destroy their populations. Species that have disappeared in recent decades include the Israel painted frog, webbed coquí, mountain mist frog, and Australian gastric brooding frog. Frogs are considered to be indicator species, and as such, they reflect changes in or conditions of their environments. When too many species go extinct, or die out, scientists become concerned about the factors that led to their demise.

Scientists in Australia were some of the first to notice the widespread decline in amphibian populations in the 1980s. One Australian native, the southern corroboree frog, is found only in a small mountainous region on the far southern tip of the continent. This frog once numbered in the millions, but in recent decades, it has declined dramatically. Fewer than 100 of these frogs now

The southern corroboree frog was featured on a 2012 Australian coin for the 150th anniversary of the Melbourne Zoo.

Unlike most freshwater frogs, crab-eating frogs favor the slightly salty waters of mangrove swamps in Southeast Asia.

remain on the planet. Despite facing few natural predators and living in a legally protected habitat, the frogs have continued to disappear, stricken with chytridiomycosis, an infection from the chytrid (*KIT-rid*) fungus.

Australian biologist Will Osborne first came across the disease in 1998 while studying the decline of northern and southern corroboree frogs. The disease, which can affect all amphibians, destroys the frogs' skin. The fungus appeared in Australia about 40 years ago, but not much is known about it. The belief is that the fungus attacks an amphibian's skin cells, inhibiting respiration and slowly suffocating the animal. The disease has spread rapidly around the globe, wiping out populations of frogs in its wake. Chytrid was also identified in Kihansi spray toads in Tanzania in 1998. The disease, coupled with habitat loss, caused Kihansi spray toads to become extinct in the wild by 2003. Fortunately, 500 spray toads were sent to the Toledo and Bronx zoos for **captive-breeding** in 2000. In the U.S., the captive spray toad population grew to 6,000, and in 2011, about 1,000 frogs were returned to Tanzania as part of a reintroduction program.

The Monteverde Cloud Forest Reserve in Costa Rica is home to a rich variety of plant and animal life. In 1987, researchers found that in just 30 square miles (77.7 sq km) of forest, more than 50 amphibian species thrived. Since that time, however, about two-thirds of the 110 species of harlequin frogs have vanished. Scientists such as James P. Collins of the University of Arizona believe that **global warming** has created more favorable conditions for chytrid, which is responsible for wiping out harlequin frogs as well as many other amphibians in the mountain rainforests of Central and South America.

Chytrid fungus is also starting to affect frog populations in North America. In addition to the introduction of frog predators such as bullfrogs, fish, and crayfish not naturally found in certain frog habitats, the decline of Chiricahua leopard frogs in Mexico and the U.S. can be attributed to

Kihansi spray toads are named for their habitat: the spray zone surrounding the Kihansi waterfalls in Tanzania.

Phyllobates, a genus of poison dart frogs of South America, includes the golden dart frog, which has killed humans with its toxic skin.

The Chiricahua leopard frog has suffered the most severe population decline of any leopard frog species.

chytrid. For 15 years, the Phoenix Zoo has contributed to a recovery program for the Chiricahua leopard frog, a threatened species that, in Arizona, is native to the Mogollon Rim and the Huachuca Mountains. To alleviate the high **mortality rate** of tadpoles and froglets in the wild (less than 5 percent of which survive to adulthood), the Phoenix Zoo's Lowland Anuran Conservation Center and New Native Species Recovery Center specialize in the captive-breeding of Chiricahua leopard frogs, increasing the survival rate to more than 90 percent. Once the tadpoles are large enough, they are released into the wild, thus improving the chances of this species' recovery in its natural habitats.

Similarly, the Denver Zoo has been working with conservationists in Peru and Bolivia, home to Earth's sole wild population of Lake Titicaca frogs, the largest aquatic frog in the world. In the late 1990s, researchers observed an 80 percent drop in the number of Lake Titicaca frogs, which can reach lengths of nearly 20 inches (50.8 cm) and weights of up to 2.5 pounds (1.1 kg). In 2008, the Denver Zoo began assisting in a captive-breeding program, whose first captive Lake Titicaca frog eggs hatched in 2011.

Although none of the tadpoles survived more than two weeks, the persistent scientists believed the program was bound to achieve success eventually.

Not only are frogs disappearing, but they are also developing deformities, most of which lead to infertility and death. Non-natural substances that pollute water sources, such as agricultural fertilizers and herbicides—particularly the chemical atrazine, which was banned by the European Union but not the U.S. or Canada—are blamed for the growth of extra limbs and changes in **hormones** and reproductive organs in numerous species,

Frogs changing from tadpoles into adults are the most vulnerable to predators, since they cannot yet leap far on land.

The elegant torrent frog is under threat of losing its habitat, thanks to the presence of a hydroelectric dam.

Frogs never need to drink water because they can absorb all the moisture their bodies need directly through their skin.

including northern leopard frogs. Recent research has found that atrazine can even cause male frogs to develop female reproductive organs, thus risking the future of many frog populations. As humans continue to disturb frog habitats by draining marshes, diverting waterways, and polluting water sources, new **parasites**, diseases, and infections increasingly take their toll on frog populations.

Researchers at the University of Delhi are hopeful that frogs can continue to endure the changes to our planet. They recently launched a program called "Lost! Amphibians of India," whose aim is to rediscover approximately 50 amphibian species whose existence has not been recorded in recent decades. Many of these species are considered extinct. Researchers speculate that at least some of these elusive species, many of which are frogs, may still exist. In 2011, the program rediscovered five species previously thought to be extinct: the nocturnal Chalazodes bubble-nest frog (unrecorded since 1874) was spotted in far southern India; the Anamalai dot frog and the elegant torrent frog, both thought to have been extinct for more than 70 years; and the Dehradun stream frog and the Silent Valley tropical frog, neither of which had been previously spotted in

more than two decades. As the Lost! program continues, researchers from all around the world have joined the search for lost frogs and other amphibians in India.

Frogs are marvelous, diverse, and valuable creatures. They are vital to the health of their **ecosystems**, and they signal the health of our own environments. Frogs and their aquatic habitats are limited and often fragile resources—they can never be replaced once driven to extinction. If we want them to exist for future generations, efforts at conserving them must be undertaken today.

The Chalazodes bubble-nest frog is a secretive species that inhabits moist evergreen forests.

ANIMAL TALE: THE FROG AND THE PRONGHORN

The Kootenai Indians—of the American states of Idaho and Montana and Canada's British Columbia—have traditionally relied on big game such as pronghorn for food and other products, and they have regarded frogs as small but necessary links in the ecosystems of their northern habitats. In this Kootenai legend, the frog is a trickster, teaching a valuable lesson about equality.

Long ago, Pronghorn was very conceited, boasting to everyone, "No one is faster than I."

Frog laughed at Pronghorn and said, "You are not fast—I could beat you in a race."

This made Pronghorn angry. "I am the swiftest creature in the land," he said. "If you want a challenge, I will wager anything."

"Agree to be my slave," said Frog. "And I will wager the same."

All the animals heard this challenge and trembled in fear for Frog, whom they knew was incapable of running as fast as Pronghorn.

"I accept your challenge," Pronghorn agreed. "Tomorrow we will race."

Frog was very clever and hurried to the swamp to gather his cousins. "You will help me show Pronghorn that he should not be conceited," explained Frog to his cousins. "We all look alike, so we will each take turns hopping ahead of Pronghorn and trick him." Frog's cousins agreed, and they all set off to hide in the tall grass.

Morning came, and Pronghorn and Frog agreed to race in the tall grass from the swamp to the forest. They took off, and within seconds Pronghorn looked behind him and saw Frog hopping far behind. Pronghorn turned and looked ahead. But there was Frog, hopping with all

his might. Pronghorn passed him by, glancing over his shoulder as he left Frog in the grass. But when he turned his eyes forward again, there was Frog, just ahead of him. This continued all the way to the forest, where Pronghorn arrived to find Frog resting on a stone. "Looks like I won," Frog said.

Pronghorn was befuddled. "How did—?"

"You are not as swift as you boast," said Frog. "Care to go again?"

"Certainly!" answered Pronghorn.

Pronghorn ran faster than he had ever run before. He glanced back and saw Frog far behind. There is no way he can beat me, Pronghorn thought to himself. But when he looked up, he saw Frog hopping furiously ahead of him. Pronghorn put his head down and charged with all his might. In an instant he was far ahead of Frog. Once again, however, as he pushed closer to the finish line, he saw Frog in the distance ahead of him. Over and over he passed Frog, only to discover moments later that Frog was in the lead.

Finally, Pronghorn reached the swamp, and there was Frog, sitting on a log. "Care to go again?" he asked Pronghorn.

"Certainly not!" Pronghorn said. "I had no idea you were so swift. I am your slave, Frog."

"Nonsense," said Frog. "Being the fastest doesn't matter. Neither you nor I are any more important than all the other creatures of the land—we should work together and learn from each other."

"You are right," admitted Pronghorn. "Little frogs are just as important as mighty pronghorn." And with that, Pronghorn went back out to the prairie to practice hopping through the tall grass.

GLOSSARY

adapting – changing to improve chances of survival in an environment

aquatic – living or growing in water

camouflage – the ability to hide, due to coloring or markings that blend in with a given environment

captive-breeding – being bred and raised in a place from which escape is not possible

cultures – particular groups in a society that share behaviors and characteristics that are accepted as normal by that group

ecosystems – communities of organisms that live together in environments

fetishes – objects believed by certain cultures to embody spirits or possess magical powers

global warming – the gradual increase in Earth's temperature that causes changes in climates, or long-term weather conditions, around the world

hibernate – to spend the winter in a sleeplike state in which breathing and heart rate slow down

hormones – chemical substances produced in the body that control and regulate the activity of certain cells and organs

larvae – the newly hatched, wingless, often wormlike form of many insects before they become adults

larynx – the organ in the neck of animals that protects the throat and houses the vocal cords (folds of tissue capable of vibration) when present

membranes – thin, clear layers of tissue that cover internal organs or developing limbs

mortality rate – the number of deaths in a certain area or period

nutrients – substances that can give an animal energy and help it grow

parasites – animals or plants that live on or inside another living thing (called a host) while giving nothing back to the host; some parasites cause disease or even death

pigment – a material or substance present in the tissues of animals or plants that gives them their natural coloring

vertebrates – animals that have a backbone, including mammals, birds, reptiles, amphibians, and fish

webbed – connected by a web (of skin, as in the case of webbed feet)

SELECTED BIBLIOGRAPHY

Dorcas, Mike, and Whit Gibbons. *Frogs: The Animal Answer Guide*. Baltimore: Johns Hopkins University Press, 2011.

du Preez, Louis, and Vincent Carruthers. *A Complete Guide to the Frogs of Southern Africa*. Cape Town: Struik Nature, 2009.

Mattison, Chris. *300 Frogs: A Visual Reference to Frogs and Toads from around the World*. Buffalo, N.Y.: Firefly Books, 2007.

Mattison, Chris. *Frogs and Toads of the World*. Princeton, N.J.: Princeton University Press, 2011.

Oregon Department of Fish and Wildlife. "Frogs and Toads at Home in Oregon." http://www.dfw.state.or.us/conservationstrategy/frogs.asp.

San Diego Zoo. "Animal Bytes: Panamanian Golden Frog." http://www.sandiegozoo.org/animalbytes/t-panamanian_golden_frog.html.

The most colorful body parts of the red-eyed treefrog are thought to aid it in its ability to startle predators.

INDEX